ROCK CLIMBING

By S.L. Hamilton

Published by ABDO Publishing Company, 8000 West 78th Street, Suite 310,
Edina, MN 55439. Copyright ©2010 by Abdo Consulting Group, Inc. International
copyrights reserved in all countries. No part of this book may be reproduced
in any form without written permission from the publisher. A&D Xtreme™ is a
trademark and logo of ABDO Publishing Company.

Printed in the United States of America, North Mankato, Minnesota.
102009
012010

 PRINTED ON RECYCLED PAPER

Editor: John Hamilton
Graphic Design: Sue Hamilton
Cover Design: John Hamilton
Cover Photo: Getty Images
Interior Photos: Corbis-pgs 4, 5, 8, 9, & 29;
Getty Images-pgs 1, 6, 7, 10, 11, 12, 13, 14, 15, 18, 19, 22, 23, 24, 25, 28, 30, & 31;
iStockphoto-pgs 2, 3, 12, 16, 20, 21, 26, & 27, ; Jupiterimages-pg 32; National
Geographic-pgs 16-17.

Library of Congress Cataloging-in-Publication Data

Hamilton, Sue L., 1959-
  Rock climbing / S.L. Hamilton.
     p. cm. -- (Xtreme sports)
  Includes index.
  ISBN 978-1-61613-003-9
  1. Rock climbing. I. Title.
  GV200.2.H355 2010
  796.522'3--dc22

                    2009037046

CONTENTS

Xtreme Climbing 4

Climbing Styles 6

Climbing Gear 18

Body Strength 24

Climbing Grades 26

Dangers and Deaths 28

The Glossary. 30

Index 32

XTREME

Extreme
climbers
defy gravity,
risking all to take
on the world's most
challenging cliffs,
mountains, and mesas.

CLIMBING

CLIMBING

STYLES

Rock climbing developed as an offshoot of mountaineering. Today, there are many styles of rock climbing. All involve skill, strength, and courage. Some use raw human power and no equipment. Others require important safety gear.

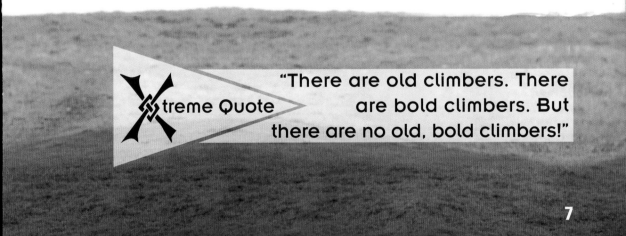

Xtreme Quote "There are old climbers. There are bold climbers. But there are no old, bold climbers!"

Bouldering

One style of rock climbing is bouldering. This challenges climbers to use their strength and wits to make intense, nearly impossible moves up a large rock. Because bouldering is done without any ropes or protective gear, the rule is to never climb higher than a person would like to fall. Usually, the boulder is from 10-16 feet (3-5 m) tall.

Xtreme Fact

Bouldering builds strength and new skills for longer roped climbs.

"The moral here is to never trust equipment, but oneself." ~Fiona Always

Free
Climbing

People who free
climb use only the
natural handholds
and footholds that
they find. They
may keep ropes
and other safety
materials with
them to use in an
emergency, but the
intent is to take on
the rock with only
their own strength
and smarts.

Trad Climbing

Traditional, or "trad," climbing means that a person climbs where there are no permanently placed bolts. The climber makes his or her own route by placing whatever devices are needed to move up a rock. The devices are then removed. Advanced technical climbing knowledge is needed to find the safest moves.

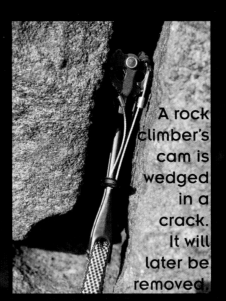

A rock climber's cam is wedged in a crack. It will later be removed.

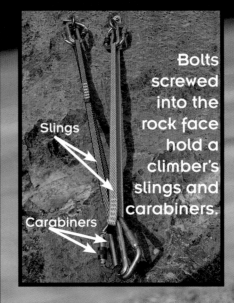

Slings

Carabiners

Bolts screwed into the rock face hold a climber's slings and carabiners.

Sport Climbing

As more people became interested in climbing for fun, the idea of sport climbing began. In this style, climbers follow routes that have been set up by others. Permanent anchors and bolts are screwed into the rock wall. Ropes may also be placed to show the route. This allows an extra degree of safety for the climber.

Xtreme Definition

"Blood /noun/ substance commonly used to mark a climbing route."

Ice Climbing

Ice climbing takes adventurers up frozen waterfalls, into ice caves, and over frozen water flows on rocks and cliffs. Ice climbers require special gear, including hand-held ice axes and front pointing crampons attached to the climbers' boots.

Crampons

Xtreme Quote

"Climbing is not a battle with the elements, nor against the law of gravity. It's a battle against oneself." ~Walter Bonatti

CLIMBING

Chalk
Bag

Carabiners

Cord

Offset Nuts

Helmet

Cams

GEAR

A climber may gear up with a helmet, harness, and climbing shoes. Additionally, rope, anchors, chalk bag, cams, carabiners, offset nuts, a belaying device, and other specialized equipment may be used.

What to Wear

One of the most important pieces of equipment is a rock climber's shoes. The smooth rubber shoe is extra tight, acting like a protective second skin around the foot. Climbers choose clothing based on how hot or cold it is where they are ascending. All climbers wear comfortable clothing that allows freedom of movement.

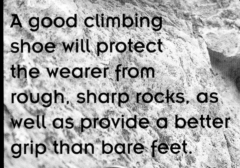

A good climbing shoe will protect the wearer from rough, sharp rocks, as well as provide a better grip than bare feet.

Comfortable clothing that moves with the climber is important.

Cold weather climbing requires heavier boots and warm clothing that still allows for freedom of movement.

Indoor rock walls allow climbers to choose an easier or a more challenging route.

Indoor Climbing

Beginners often learn to climb on indoor rock walls. Safety harnesses keep the unskilled safe while they learn. Experienced climbers use indoor rock walls to maintain and improve their skills. Especially during cold, wet weather, indoor climbing offers an athlete a good chance to work out.

23

BODY

Climbing requires great strength in a person's arms, legs, back, fingers, and toes. Climbers must be able to hold their own weight, sometimes from the smallest handhold. Climbers also need rubbery flexibility and great stamina.

STRENGTH

CLIMBING

El Capitan, in Yosemite National Park.

Climbs are graded by how long they take to complete, and by their difficulty. North America mostly follows the Yosemite Decimal System (YDS). In YDS, Class 1 is a walk. The most difficult technical rock climbing is rated Class 5.

GRADES

"Class 1: You fall, you're stupid.
Class 2: You fall, you break your arm.
Class 3: You fall, you break your leg.
Class 4: You fall, you are almost dead.
Class 5: You fall, you are dead."

~R.J. Secor

DANGERS

Climbing is dangerous.
People make mistakes
or equipment fails.
Rescues are difficult
and at times impossible.
But like any risky sport,
people who use their
brains, as well as their
muscles, live to climb
again.

AND RISKS

Xtreme Quote

"Mountains are not fair or unfair, they are just dangerous." ~Reinhold Messner

Belaying Device

A piece of climbing equipment that secures a climber while rappelling, or sliding down, a cliff. How loosely or tightly the climber grips the belay device determines how quickly or slowly he or she slides down the rope. A belay device is also used with a partner to secure a climber as he or she climbs up.

Bolt

An anchor that is pounded or drilled into rock to help a climber move up or down. This does damage the rock, so it is used as a last resort. Some sport climbing areas have permanent bolts set up on the rock face.

Cam

A metal device that fits into cracks and crevices in a rock wall to which a rope can be threaded to secure a climber. Climbers also clip to cams using a carabiner.

GLOSSARY

Carabiner
A strong, metal link with a spring-loaded opening that climbers clip onto various pieces of safety equipment.

Mesa
A flat-topped hill or mountain with steep sides.

Mountaineering
The sport of climbing mountains.

Offset Nuts
Metal devices of varying size with a rope-like handhold. The metal "nut" is designed to be jammed deep into cracks in a rock wall. This provides a climber with an extra handhold.

Sling
Strong, webbed nylon material sewn or tied into a loop. Also called a runner.

INDEX

A
Always, Fiona 10
anchors 14, 19

B
belaying device 19
blood 15
bolts 12, 14
Bonatti, Walter 17
bouldering 8, 9

C
cams 12, 18, 19
carabiners 12, 18, 19
chalk bag 18, 19
climbing shoes 19, 20
cord 18
crampons 16

E
El Capitan 26

F
free climbing 11

H
harness 19
helmet 18, 19

I
ice axes 16
ice climbing 16

M
Messner, Reinhold 29
mountaineering 7

N
North America 26

O
offset nuts 18, 19

R
rock walls 22, 23
rope 14, 19

S
safety harness 23
Secor, R.J. 27
slings 12
sport climbing 14

T
trad climbing (*See* traditional climbing)
traditional climbing 12

Y
Yosemite Decimal System (YDS) 26
Yosemite National Park 26